Black Spiny-Tailed Iguana
Lizard Lightning!

by Natalie Lunis

Consultant: Dr. Kenneth L. Krysko
Senior Biological Scientist, Division of Herpetology
Florida Museum of Natural History, University of Florida

BEARPORT
PUBLISHING

NEW YORK, NEW YORK

Credits

Cover, © Jan Ševčík; TOC, © Zach Holmes/Alamy; 4–5, © Luke Mahler; 6T, © D. Ross Cameron/Oakland Tribune/ZUMA Press/Newscom; 6C, © J. C. Carton/Bruce Coleman Inc./Alamy; 6B, © Lynda Huxley/Images of Africa Photobank/Alamy; 7, © Catherine A. Smith; 9, © Andy Jones/Cleveland Museum of Natural History; 10, © David Knowles/Dalyn Digital Photography; 11, © Ken Thomas; 12L, © William Flaxington; 12TR, © Lynn M. Stone/NaturePL/SuperStock; 12BR, © Kenneth L. Krysko; 13, © Andy Jones/Cleveland Museum of Natural History; 14, © Patricio Robles Gil/npl/Minden Pictures; 15, © Luke Mahler; 16, © Kenneth L. Krysko; 17, © Jack Hynes; 18T, © James Gerholdt/Peter Arnold Images/Photolibrary; 18B, © Bill Hubick; 19, © Joe McDonald/Animals Animals Enterprises; 20, © Jan Ševčík; 21, © Joe Cavaretta/Sun-Sentinel/ZUMA Press/Newscom; 22, © Larry Benvenuti/Graeme Teague Photography; 23TL, © Ken Thomas; 23TR, © Carolyne Pehora/Shutterstock; 23BL, © ben44/Shutterstock; 23BR, © Kenneth L. Krysko.

Publisher: Kenn Goin
Editorial Director: Adam Siegel
Creative Director: Spencer Brinker
Design: Debrah Kaiser
Photo Researcher: Omni-Photo Communications, Inc.

Special thanks to Jonathan Losos, Museum of Comparative Zoology, Harvard University

Library of Congress Cataloging-in-Publication Data

Lunis, Natalie.
  Black spiny-tailed iguana : lizard lightning! / by Natalie Lunis.
    p. cm. — (Blink of an eye : superfast animals)
  Includes bibliographical references and index.
  ISBN-13: 978-1-936087-91-4 (library binding)
  ISBN-10: 1-936087-91-X (library binding)
  1. Ctenosaura similis—Juvenile literature. I. Title.
  QL666.L25L86 2010
  597.95'42—dc22

                            2010019671

For more information, write to Bearport Publishing Company, Inc., 101 Fifth Avenue, Suite 6R, New York, New York 10003. Printed in the United States of America in North Mankato, Minnesota.

072010
042110CGE

10 9 8 7 6 5 4 3 2 1

Contents

Run, Reptile, Run! 4

Meet the Family 6

Where in the World? 8

Soaking Up the Sun 10

Run for Your Life! 12

Running for Cover 14

A Prickly Tail 16

Reptile Runner-Ups 18

Reptile Racetracks 20

Built for Speed 22

Glossary 23

Index 24

Read More 24

Learn More Online 24

About the Author 24

Run, Reptile, Run!

The black spiny-tailed iguana is the fastest **reptile** in the world.

It can run at a speed of up to 21.7 miles per hour (35 kph).

That's a lot faster than most people can run.

An Australian freshwater crocodile can run at a top speed of 11 miles per hour (18 kph). A snake called the black mamba can slither at a top speed of 12 miles per hour (19 kph). A black spiny-tailed iguana is faster than both.

Australian Freshwater Crocodile
11 mph / 18 kph

Black Mamba
12 mph / 19 kph

Black Spiny-Tailed Iguana
21.7 mph / 35 kph

Meet the Family

There are about 40 kinds of iguanas.

The best-known kind is the green iguana.

These reptiles are sometimes kept as pets.

Black spiny-tailed iguanas are also kept as pets, though much less often than green iguanas are.

Some pet owners say that black spiny-tails are harder to handle and tame than their green cousins.

green iguana

black spiny-tailed iguana

All iguanas belong to a larger group of reptiles called lizards. Some other kinds of lizards are chameleons, geckos, and monitor lizards.

chameleon

monitor lizard

Where in the World?

Until recently, black spiny-tailed iguanas were found in the wild only at the edges of dry forests in Mexico and Central America.

Now there are some also living in Florida.

Some of these iguanas are pets that escaped or were let go by their owners.

Others are the offspring, or young, of these iguanas.

Black Spiny-Tailed Iguanas in the Wild

● **Where black spiny-tailed iguanas live**

Black spiny-tailed iguanas can grow to be four feet (1.2 m) long. In Florida, because of their large size, the iguanas are sometimes mistaken for small alligators.

Soaking Up the Sun

In their forest homes, black spiny-tailed iguanas spend the night in a retreat, or hiding place.

In the morning, they come out to warm up in the sun.

The iguanas need to do so because, like all reptiles, they are **cold-blooded**.

If they do not soak up heat from the sun, they will not have the energy they need to move around and find food.

The scientific word for cold-blooded is *ectothermic*. Cold-blooded, or ectothermic, animals do not make their own heat. Instead, their body temperature rises or drops depending on the amount of heat they get from the environment.

Run for Your Life!

Adult spiny-tails don't need to run fast to get food.

That's because they eat mostly plants.

The long-tailed lizards need to reach top speed for another reason.

They zoom off to get away from jaguars, snakes, hawks, owls, and other animals that try to eat them.

jaguar

snake

owls

Like many kinds of iguanas, black spiny-tails start out eating insects. As the young iguanas grow up, however, they switch to eating plants.

13

Running for Cover

Spiny-tailed iguanas can run fast, but they can do so for only a short time before tiring out.

When one is chased by an enemy, it tries to dive back into its retreat or another safe spot, such as a space between rocks.

If the enemy keeps coming after it, the iguana tries to defend itself by lashing out with its long tail.

It might also try to bite or scratch its attacker.

When a black spiny-tailed iguana reaches a high speed, it sometimes lifts the front part of its body off the ground and runs only on its back legs.

A Prickly Tail

The black spiny-tailed iguana got part of its name from the black markings on its body.

It got another part of its name from the needle-like **spines**, or points, on its tail.

The spines help the iguana defend itself as it swings its tail to strike an enemy.

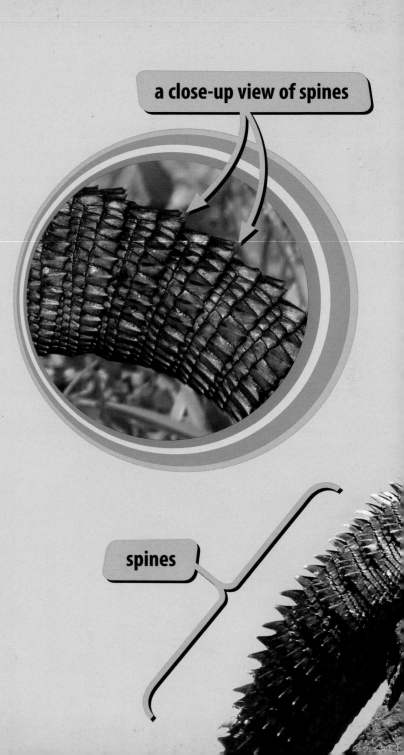

a close-up view of spines

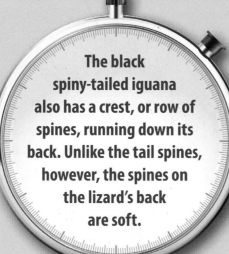

spines

The black spiny-tailed iguana also has a crest, or row of spines, running down its back. Unlike the tail spines, however, the spines on the lizard's back are soft.

crest

Reptile Runner-Ups

The black spiny-tailed iguana sets the record as the world's fastest reptile—but does it have any competition?

A lizard called the six-lined racerunner holds the record as the second-fastest sprinter.

It can reach a top speed of 18 miles per hour (29 kph).

The zebra-tailed lizard can move about as fast.

Perhaps the most amazing runner, however, is the basilisk lizard.

It can run on top of water!

six-lined racerunner

zebra-tailed lizard

As a basilisk lizard runs on a pond or stream, it slaps the water with its feet, forming bubbles of air just underneath them. These bubbles hold the lizard up and keep it from sinking—though only if it keeps moving very quickly.

basilisk lizard

Reptile Racetracks

Black spiny-tailed iguanas are shy creatures.

So how do scientists know how fast these reptiles can run?

They build special treadmills and running tracks and then use them to time the animals.

Scientists have plans to keep testing the speeds of different reptiles.

Some day they might find a runner that is even faster than the black spiny-tailed iguana.

Until that happens, however, this reptile rules!

Sometimes scientists bring equipment with them so that they can test the speed of iguanas and other lizards in the places where they live. Other times the scientists capture the animals and take them back to laboratories in order to study them.

Built for Speed

What makes a black spiny-tailed iguana run so fast? Here is how different parts of the lizard's body help it reach its amazing speeds.

long tail helps with balance while running—especially when changing direction

back legs are strong and muscular; sometimes the iguana rises up and runs only on them

front legs are shorter than back legs; along with the front of the body, they lift off the ground when the iguana starts a two-legged run

cold-blooded (*kohld*-BLUHD-id) having a body temperature that rises and drops depending on how much heat the animal gets from the environment

lizards (LIZ-urdz) types of reptiles with scaly bodies and tails; they are closely related to snakes

reptile (REP-tile) a cold-blooded animal that usually has dry, scaly skin, such as a lizard or alligator

spines (SPYENZ) sharp points

Index

basilisk lizard 18–19

Central America 8

cold-blooded 10–11

crest 16–17

enemies 12, 14, 16

Florida 8–9

food 10, 12–13

green iguana 6

homes 8, 10

lizards 6–7, 12, 16, 18–19, 21

Mexico 8

pets 6, 8

reptile 4, 6, 10, 18, 20

scientists 20–21

six-lined racerunner 18

size 9

speed 4–5, 12, 14–15, 18, 20–21, 22

spines 16

tail 14, 16, 22

zebra-tailed lizard 18

Read More

Buckingham, Suzanne. *Meet the Iguana.* New York: Rosen (2009).

Lunis, Natalie. *Green Iguanas (Peculiar Pets).* New York: Bearport (2010).

Murray, Julie. *Iguanas.* Edina, MN: ABDO (2003).

Learn More Online

To learn more about iguanas, visit
www.bearportpublishing.com/BlinkofanEye

About the Author

Natalie Lunis has written many science and nature books for children. She lives in the Hudson River Valley, just north of New York City.